DOING
OUR
PART

DOING OUR PART

AMERICAN WOMEN ON THE HOME FRONT DURING WORLD WAR II

BY SUSAN SINNOTT

A First Book
Franklin Watts
New York / Chicago / London / Toronto / Sydney

Excerpts from letters unless otherwise noted are from *Since You Went Away: World War II Letters from American Women on the Home Front,* by Judy Litoff and David C. Smith, eds., Oxford University Press, 1991.

Cover art by Jane Sterrett

Photographs copyright ©: Archive Photos/Lambert: pp. 2, 14, 25, 39; Wide World Photos: pp. 8, 42, 43; State Historical Society of Wisconsin: p. 10; The National Archives: pp. 12, 34, 48; UPI/Bettmann: pp. 16, 32, 51, 56, 57; U.S. Air Force Museum: p. 20; Archive Photos: pp. 22 (Welgos), 24, 36, 44; Archives of Labor and Urban Affairs, Wayne State University: p. 28; Minnesota Historical Society: p. 30; The Bettmann Archive: p. 49.

Library of Congress Cataloging-in-Publication Data

Susan Sinnott.
    Doing our part : American women on the home front during World War II / by Susan Sinnott.
        p. cm. — (A First book)
        Includes bibliographical references and index.
        ISBN 0-531-20198-8 (lib. bdg.)
        1. World War, 1939–1945—Women—United States. 2. World War, 1939–1945—War work—United States. 3. Women—United States—History —20th century. I. Title II. Series.
D810.W7S543 1995
940.53'15042—dc20   94-39905
                                                                  CIP
                                                                  AC

CONTENTS

DOING
OUR
PART

DON'T YOU KNOW THERE'S A WAR ON?

Atlanta, December 11, 1941

Dearest Charlie:

. . . Well, what about this WAR business? . . . A man here in the office just said that Italy had declared WAR on the U.S.A. What's going to happen to us? There is no doubt in my mind as to whom shall win this WAR, but how long will it take us? It makes you feel like getting the best of everything before it's all gone. Now I know that isn't the right way to feel, is it Charlie?

Barbara
from the book *Since You Went Away*

In September 1939, the European allies of the United States went to war against Germany and Italy, and America was struggling to over-

come its decade-long economic depression. During 1940, France fell to Hitler's army, and America's shipyards, aircraft plants, and munitions factories began to respond with a modest effort to help in Europe's defense. But, only after the Japanese bombed Pearl Harbor on December 7, 1941, and the United States entered the war in both Europe and the Pacific, did the government undertake a massive spending effort to move the American economy into full-scale war production.

Suddenly a nation that, only a few months before, had agonized over a 20 percent unemployment rate now needed to fill an unprecedented demand for new workers to fuel this wartime economy. With our allies in Europe struggling to simply hold on to their homelands, the United States set out to become the arsenal of democracy—that is, the supplier of arms that would defend the free world.

At the same time, however, that the United States was manufacturing the ships, planes, and weapons for the war, we were also sending soldiers by the boatload to the battlefronts. Who, then, would become the home-front production soldiers America and its allies so badly needed? As men headed into military service, both industry and the U.S. government realized they would have to

This Great Lakes shipyard in Manitowoc, Wisconsin, was one of the many that geared up in 1941 to meet the demands of war production.

turn to the "ones left behind"—the women—to do their part by taking over these vital jobs.

This policy decision was problematic, however, since it was the exact opposite of the one encouraged during the Great Depression of the 1930s. Because of the scarcity of work during that decade, women had been urged to stay at home and let men take whatever jobs were available. The idea that married women were first *house*wives had become deeply ingrained in the American psyche and would not be easily changed.

Yet women of all ages, married and unmarried, answered the government's call. Just before the start of World War II, women made up 25 percent of the American labor force. By 1944 that figure had grown to 36 percent as 5 million women entered the work force. One occupation more than any other became linked in the public's mind with the new woman worker: riveter. These workers helped assemble the tens of thousands of military airplanes needed in the war effort. Riveters often worked in pairs, with one person using a special gun to shoot the rivet into the metal and another person bucking, or flattening, it. The huge number of riveters needed

Thousands of women took jobs as riveters in airplane factories. The popular song "Rosie the Riveter" helped create the image of workers who could do men's jobs while remaining completely feminine.

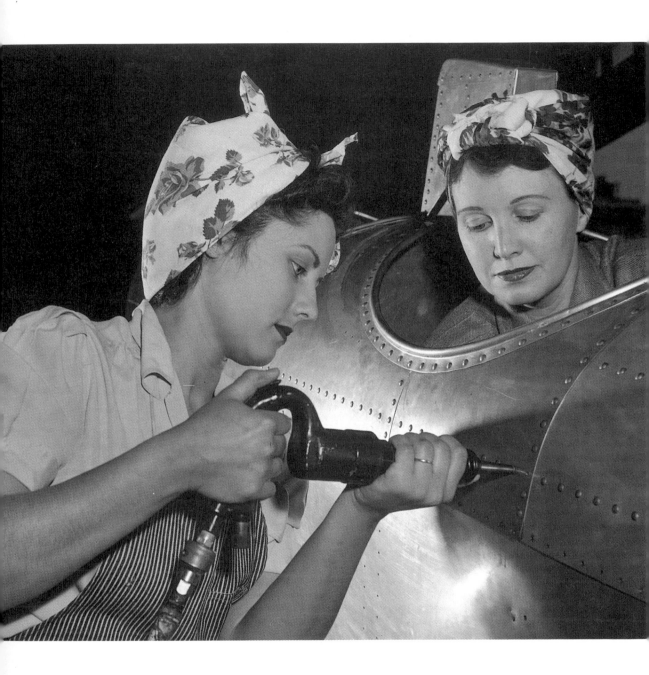

by the airplane manufacturers gave rise to the icon of "Rosie the Riveter." As pictured in the famous poster, Rosie combined strong muscles, an iron will, and a pretty face. Her picture with the hearty caption "We can do it!" became the most enduring image we have of women on the home front during World War II.

But, as always, there's a real story behind the myth. Even as women were urged to fill these worthy jobs by government or business, they were also expected to remain housewives and mothers. No one else would take on the demands of running a household and caring for children. The fact was that, even though women were being called to fill men's jobs, they could not give up their other responsibilities.

Despite all the posters, radio spots, and other advertising designed to make war jobs seem noble and patriotic, public opinion was never really on the side of working women. This was especially true for married women with young children. Husbands, at home or on the battlefront, often were skeptical that factory work wouldn't somehow make their wives less womanly. Newspaper writers added to this impression. The well-known columnist Max Lerner led the way when he wrote that the war was creating a "new Amazon." Women

Riveters usually worked in pairs. Here one woman shoots a rivet into an airplane's cockpit while the other waits to flatten it.

Newspaper columnist Max Lerner was one of many in the media who questioned whether women could take on war work without losing their femininity.

found themselves caught between their duty to home and their duty to country; no matter which they chose, armchair critics were ready to pounce on them. And while many thousands of American women marched happily off to work, their jobs eventually took a great toll and the women who tried to "do it all" were left exhausted and demoralized.

Pensacola, June 8, 1944

Darlin',

. . . After I get settled in Louisville I'm thinking seriously of going to work in some defense plant there on the swing shift so I can be at home during the day with Bill [their young son] as he needs me—would like to know what you think of the idea. . . . I can't save anything by not working and I want to have something for us when you get home so you can enjoy life for a while before going back to work and Bill and I want all of your time too for a while so's we can all three make up for lost time.

Gotta scoot as I have several more chores to do. . . . Polly

from *Since You Went Away*

WANTED: PRODUCTION SOLDIERS

Darlin',

You are now the husband of a career woman—just call me your little Ship Yard Babe! Yeh! I made up my mind that I wanted to work from 4:00 P.M. 'till midnight so's I could have my cake and eat it too. I wanted to work but didn't want to leave Bill all day. . .

. . . Opened my little checking account too and it's a grand and glorious feeling to write a check all your own and not have to ask for one. . . . I'm gonna start sockin' it in the savings and checking too so's we'll have something when our sweet little Daddy comes home.

Good nite, Darlin'
I love you, Polly

The importance of the United States' ability to produce planes, ships, and weapons for the war simply can't be understated. This war, which had engulfed the entire globe, would not be won by the side that could send the most men into battle. Military hardware and machinery would decide this conflict. Consequently, in 1941, President Franklin D. Roosevelt called for U.S. aircraft factories to produce 50,000 planes a year, even though these same plants had built only a few thousand in 1940.

Seemingly overnight, auto factories were converted to exclusively military uses, shipyards were expanded, and munitions plants were built all over the country. The nation's industrial base, which had been sluggish during the Depression years of the 1930s, dramatically switched into high gear. As the factories and shipyards retooled and expanded, however, both government and industry became aware of the acute need for so-called "production soldiers." Ten million men boarded ships bound for Europe and the Pacific, and the country realized, as one magazine editor wrote, that the manpower problem was instead "a problem in woman power."

The "woman problem" was complicated, however. Both government and industry leaders recognized the obstacles to hiring large numbers of women who had previously not worked outside the home. In 1936, in the midst of the Great Depression, a public opinion poll found that 82 percent of all Americans believed wives with employed husbands should not work outside the home.

Industry and government leaders now needed to convince these same women that they should leave their families and homes and perform tasks that were considered very masculine indeed.

Further complicating a woman's decision was the fact that housework was then much more demanding than it is today. In 1941, one-third of American women cooked not with gas or electricity but with wood or coal; this involved a great investment of time and energy. Running water, so common today that we scarcely give it a thought, was not always available, and water often had to be carried from an outside source, making laundry a backbreaking chore. In fact, at the beginning of the 1940s, both farm and city women spent fifty hours each week on household duties. Wartime shortages and rationing added extra time and frustration to a woman's housework.

To achieve its goal of replacing male workers with female workers, therefore, the U.S. government had no choice but to crank up its propaganda machine. American women had to be persuaded, or coerced, into believing that the good of the country had to come before either their own or their family's convenience. Not surprisingly,

By mid-1941 airplane production was in high gear. Here newly manufactured Curtiss P-40 fighter planes sit at Ohio's Patterson Field waiting to be sent into battle overseas.

Housework in the early 1940s was more demanding than it is today. Many homes still didn't have indoor plumbing, so water had to be carried from an outside source with pails and buckets.

radio and print advertisements appealed first to a woman's emotions. The ads argued that the least women could do to save the lives of husbands, boyfriends, and brothers was to get war jobs. "Be the woman behind the man behind the gun," the ads urged. "Victory is in your hands." Songs such as "Rosie the Riveter," which turned a young woman worker with a boyfriend in the marines into a symbol of national heroism, were heard everywhere.

Magazines joined the campaign, too, as they mixed patriotism and glamour. One publication, the *Woman's Home Companion*, took four women workers to Hollywood for fashion and hair makeovers. They were then photographed to show how defense plant workers could be just as beautiful as any other women. The article explained carefully that even these women who did men's work—and had the dirty overalls and fingernails to prove it—could become as glamorous as any movie star when their workday was over. The motion picture industry in Hollywood also pressed the cause, producing films that featured famous stars going to work each morning in drab slacks. They, of course, never looked anything less than beautiful and radiant.

Such campaigns went a long way toward persuading students and single women to join up, but they had little effect on housewives. Many had very young children who needed to be cared for during the day. Wasn't it enough, they wondered, for wives and mothers to participate in salvage drives, buy war bonds, do Red Cross work, and plant Victory Gardens? Could they really rely on other fam-

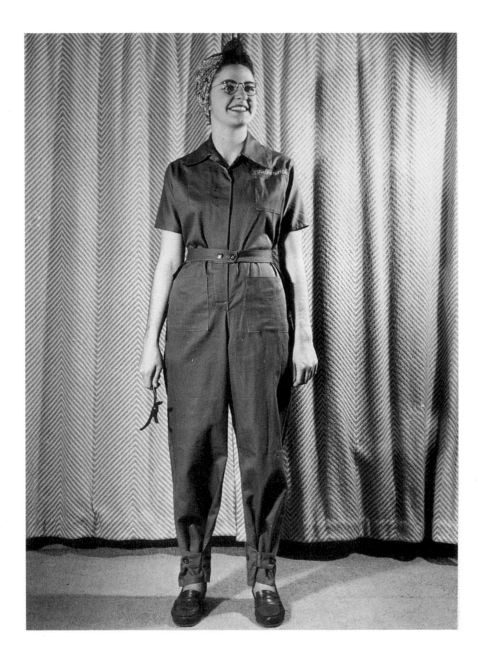

The U.S. government encouraged Americans to grow and preserve their own food in backyard or community garden plots. These so-called Victory Gardens became familiar sites throughout the country.

Many women's magazines photographed war workers to prove to readers that taking such jobs wouldn't make them unattractive.

ily members to help with the house and children, or would they need to use paid help? And how would their husbands react to their war work? Many men were thoroughly convinced by the Depression-era attitude that a woman's place was in the home, and they regarded their wives' jobs as a slight against their manhood.

Because of these attitudes, a different advertising campaign was planned for married women with children. The messages appealed to their domestic sides, especially to the self-sacrifice that had helped get their families through the difficult Depression years. The government even suggested that the skills used in the home were similar to those needed for defense work. Running a drill press or rivet gun, one brochure suggested, was no different from operating a sewing machine. This propaganda broke through the initial hesitancy and led more and more "Mrs. Stay-at-Homes," as they were called, to take war jobs. By 1944, when war production was at its height and 120,000 planes were being produced, one in three women working in the defense industry was a wife and mother. These former homemakers, who turned their lives upside down to do their part, captured the public imagination and were glorified—at first, anyway—as home-front heroines.

DOING THEIR PART

I'm a housewife, too, although I never worked out-side my home until this year. Feeding my family and buying war bonds just didn't seem like enough. So I got an 8-hour-a-week day job and managed to run my home besides. My husband's proud of me . . . and I've never been happier.

Government-sponsored radio spots, such as this one, aired frequently, especially in areas near Seattle, Detroit, and Norfolk, Virginia, where defense-related industries needed to find thousands of workers for their huge plants. In Seattle, where there were several defense plants, a four-week radio campaign helped recruit 2,200 women workers. Detroit auto facto-ries, which had quickly converted to war production, sent employment registration forms to 500,000 households in surrounding Wayne County. This campaign alone resulted

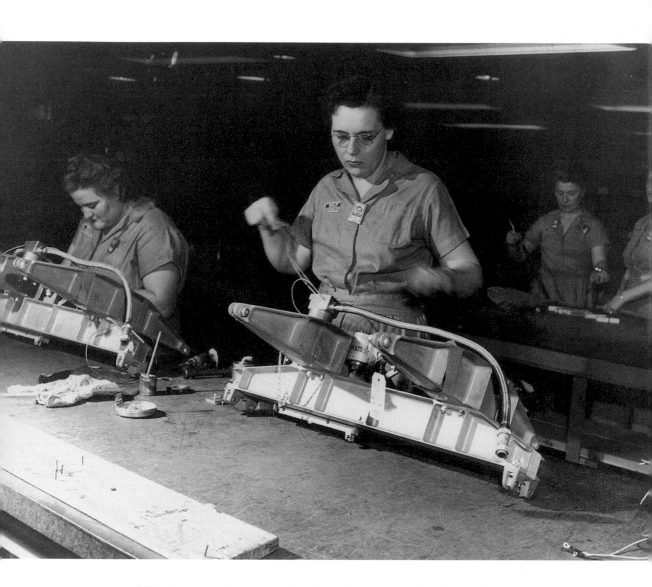

Workers make parts for bombers at a De Soto factory in Detroit, Michigan, a city that drew job seekers from rural parts of the Midwest and South.

in 142,000 new women employees. When asked on a registration card to explain why she wanted to work, one woman wrote, "My husband is in Australia and I want to make weapons for him and his buddies."

Most women took jobs close to home. Those who lived near centers of war production had no trouble doing their patriotic duty, if they chose to. Those who lived in rural areas, however, often had no such opportunity—unless, of course, they moved, which they did in large numbers. Many left the hills of West Virginia and North Carolina, for example, to work in the shipyards along the Atlantic coast. Other women traveled from quiet farms in Missouri and Arkansas to Los Angeles, San Diego, and Detroit, where they found high-paying jobs. As this migration, with its strains on resources and energy, threatened to cost America too dearly during a time of shortages and rationing, the U.S. government tried to discourage the large-scale relocation of workers.

Government officials tried to stress instead that employment should come from locally available labor. "Locally available," however, also implied "locally willing." If women weren't willing to leave home and find jobs, was it in the nation's interest to force them to work? A national debate began about the possibility of forcing women to work. It quickly became heated. The magazine *Business Week* stated its opinion in its cover headline: "Draft for Women." ("Draft" in this case meant compulsory civilian work.) There was serious debate, too, in the U.S. Congress but the matter never actually came to a vote.

Perhaps one of the reasons women, and especially

housewives, didn't enter the workforce immediately was that basic changes in industry were needed to make war jobs more attractive to them. One fundamental change had to be equal pay for equal work. Industry had long set aside a few jobs for women, but these were always the lowest-paying positions. The federal government now realized that if it were going to ask women to take over men's jobs, the women would need to earn the same wages as a man. Public sentiment supported this notion, as did government statements, but no legislation was passed to make the equity principle stick. (The Equal Pay Act did not pass the U.S. Congress until 1963.) Instead, pay equity varied from industry to industry and from plant to plant.

Among the leaders in providing high wages and good working conditions for women was the newest industry, aircraft manufacturing. Hundreds of thousands of workers—nearly one-half million by 1943—who had never even seen a plane close up, flocked to Douglas, Boeing, and Martin Aircraft, to name a few. At these plants women made up half of the workforce, replacing men who had gone to war while at the same time helping

The government tried to gently nudge women into war work. A debate raged, however, about whether they should indeed be drafted, or forced, to take such jobs.

These workers give a final inspection to
airplane propellers that have just come
off a mass-production line.

the country meet its commitment to double its defense output.

The aircraft industry was new at the time and didn't have the a traditional all-male workforce and so it was willing to establish innovative training programs for women. The industry seemed to recognize that inexperienced muscles would need more rest and that safety and cleanliness were key issues. Some of the most forward-thinking labor policies of the time came, in fact, from the prodding of the female workers.

To be sure, there was nothing easy about defense work. Aircraft plants were as big as small towns, and the noise of constant production was nerve-racking. Muscles became sore and hands swollen. One worker described the stressful work of riveting inside a plane's nose cone: "Two riveters would be screaming through the skin of the plane to give each other instructions. Their gun would go off, screeching hollowly into my eardrums. There would be two men hammering on the outside just over my head." Backaches and headaches were common and many workers had trouble sleeping as the noise continued to throb throughout their bodies even when they were at home.

Shipyards, unlike aircraft plants, were accustomed to all-male workforces and were slower to accept women, despite government pressures. In 1940, one hundred thousand workers were employed in these yards, and all but thirty-six of them were men. By 1943, however, there was a demand for 1.5 million shipyard workers. Clearly, America's shipbuilding needs, especially after such naval

disasters as the bombing of Pearl Harbor, were so great the shipyards were forced to hire women.

Even though shipbuilders did undertake training programs, they clearly regarded the women as temporary workers. In shipbuilding, however, as with aircraft manufacturing, women found that skills previously considered "just" domestic made them well qualified for many tasks. One former housewife put it this way: "It's really simple to build a ship . . . you get your plan, cut out your pattern, prefabricate it, fit it together and launch it. Men have always made such a deal out of it!"

One example often cited was the similarity women found between cutting out patterns for clothes and for ships. The only difference was that ships were made of steel rather than cloth! Women also excelled at welding and at operating drill presses, grinders, and lathes. In general, however, they considered shipyards less desirable workplaces than aircraft plants. Airplane workers might have had to endure incessant noise, but shipyard workers were exposed to the natural elements as they worked on the edge of the water. Their work could also be extremely dangerous. One woman riveter recalled that on her first day on the job she had to climb a high scaf-

Short vocational classes taught former waitresses, secretaries, and housewives the skills they needed to build ships and make airplanes.

folding to complete her rivets. Before heading up she nervously asked her boss whether people often fell to the concrete below. "Not often," he replied acidly. "Just once."

Women also achieved considerable success in many other industries, including munitions manufacturing, where they loaded shells and made fuses. They worked in the steel industry, too, filling twenty different job categories where before only one had been open to them. Their success in these essential areas of war productions was best summed up by Donald Nelson, chairman of the War Production Board:

> This is the record: for nine years before Pearl Harbor, Germany, Italy, and Japan prepared intensively for war, while as late as 1940 the war production of peaceful America was virtually nothing. Yet two years later the output of our war factories equaled that of the Axis nations combined. In 1943 our war production was one and one half times, and in 1944, more than double Axis war production—a remarkable demonstration of power.

Women workers were particularly successful in munitions manufacturing, where they loaded shells and made fuses.

A DELICATE
BALANCE

The presence of so many women in industry was soon reflected in the popular tunes America listened to: "The Lady at Lockheed," "We're the Janes Who Make the Planes," and, of course, "Rosie the Riveter." The working women were sometimes surprised, however, to find that working conditions were not as good as the happy, friendly lyrics of these songs suggested. Also, because they believed the government propaganda, women thought they were doing their patriotic duty by working and that friends, neighbors, and indeed, the nation would understand the sacrifices they were making. They expected, in other words, to be welcomed.

In nearly all cases, however—aircraft plants being an exception—women were heading into an all-male do-

Women often found that the difficult, dangerous nature of war work was at odds with the happy, upbeat lyrics of popular songs and advertisements.

main. They were expected not only to dress like men and work like men, but to "take it like a man" as well. And take it they did, particularly from older male workers who resented their very presence. These colleagues were all too often convinced that they couldn't do the job. Many men clung to this belief no matter how much proof women offered to the contrary. A common thought among these men was "She didn't, and even if she did, she couldn't have."

When management ignored this problem, as it often did, women decided to gain respect the only way they could—by outperforming men. The fact that they did this again and again was a result of the determination and time-management skills they had brought to the work-place from the home. At home they never had to "look busy" or fool others into thinking their work was done while they watched the clock. Neither was there a time clock or a supervisor at home; there was simply self-discipline, which women were able to use to great advantage.

Now more than ever, women needed these time management skills, both at home and at work. A typical war job might involve a six-day, forty-eight hour week, leaving just one day off. The pressure placed on home-makers by rationing and shortages meant long trips and long lines to buy basic staples. Combined work and home responsibilities looked daunting by any measure. "All over the country," wrote one newspaper reporter, "mothers of young children seemed too exhausted to talk about their work. If they did talk to me I hadn't the heart to take much of their time or energy. "

There was little leeway in any working woman's schedule. Commuting time varied, of course, but two hours a day was not unusual. With both gas and tires subject to rationing, very few workers could simply drive to work each morning. They needed to rely instead on either public transportation or ride sharing. "The chief discombobulation to my life," said one woman, "is rising in the dark at five, going twenty miles, picking up riders, and reporting ready for work at five minutes to seven."

Schedules were even more hectic for the women who worked at night. They usually finished work at 6:00 or 7:00 A.M. and immediately went to buy rationed meat before it ran out. They arrived home in time to make breakfast for their children and send them off to school. Then it was time for a few hours' sleep, after setting the alarm for 11:30 A.M. to be ready when the children came home for lunch at noon. When lunch was over and the dishes cleared, it was back to bed until just before 3:00 P.M., when the children came home from school. Sleep wasn't even a possibility as the night worker did her housework, made dinner, kissed her family good night, and headed off to work, which began again at 10:00 P.M.

As loud as the media cry had been for women to pitch in for the war effort, there was not a word about what to do when two full-time jobs—worker and housewife—seemed too much to bear. As fatigue and illness became common, women workers were criticized by

A typical shopping trip for rationed products often involved waiting in long lines like this one in New York City. Patience could often be in short supply for the weary war worker.

employers and the media because of absenteeism. Only a few sensitive observers realized that many women had simply reached the breaking point:

> Home-making minutiae are distracting and energy-draining. When household equipment needs replacement, when the children's shoe size changes, when the toothpaste runs out, it is Mother and not Father who scribbles memoranda on scraps of paper and squeezes in the necessary shopping sometime, somewhere. . . . If a woman can learn to run a drill press, why can't a man learn to run a washing machine?

> From "America's Pampered Husbands," *The Nation*, July 10, 1943

Homemaking for women with war jobs, especially those who worked at night, was hectic and tiring. War workers had little in common with the "ideal housewife" portrayed in women's magazines.

NOT JUST A HOUSEWIFE

As difficult as the lives of the hundreds of thousands of "Rosies" might have been, there were many stresses placed on those who remained "average" housewives as well. With fifteen million American men fighting overseas, many women were both mother and father, household head and servant. The fact was there was nothing normal about the war years, and nothing ordinary about its routine tasks, either.

On the morning after the Japanese bombed Pearl Harbor, Hawaii, shoppers streamed into their local groceries and stripped the shelves bare. The first item to run out was sugar, one of Hawaii's main exports. Many people had vivid memories of World War I, when no one could count on the availability of various staples from one week to the next. As soon as President Roosevelt declared war on Japan on December 7, 1941, those same people began to hoard goods. As a result, supplies dropped suddenly and prices rose rapidly.

A system of rationing was soon imposed. Though viewed initially by many as a left-wing plot, rationing soon won public approval despite its inconveniences. People realized the cumbersome system helped keep prices at reasonable levels and assured that scarce goods would be available not only to the privileged but to all who had at least a degree of patience. Women quickly learned the baffling system, grasping the difference between certificate rationing, coupon rationing, and value points.

Sugar rationing, for example, began on May 5, 1942. Each family was given coupons that allowed them to buy one pound of sugar a week, although a quarter of that was withheld for special supplements for home canning, holidays, and restaurants. If people grumbled that they needed more sugar, they were reminded that Hawaii's precious sugarcane was also used to make molasses, which was needed to produce the ethyl alcohol needed in gun powder, torpedo fuel, and dynamite. Sugar for morning coffee wasn't *that* important, given the entire intricate picture.

Coffee, meat, and dairy products were also rationed, not because production was disturbed, but to prevent hoarding. In 1943 a public opinion poll was published that listed the goods people found the hardest to give up.

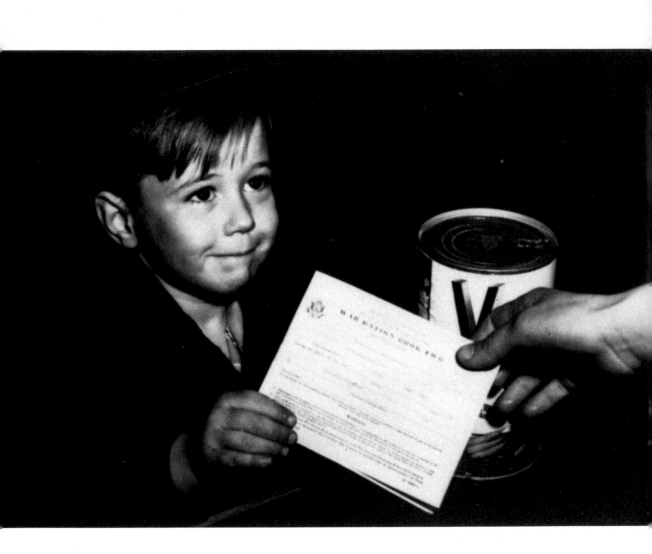

Rationing, which began in 1942, seemed complicated at first but soon became a normal part of daily life.

Women here register for sugar coupons, which will allow them to buy one pound of sugar a week. Rationing assured that scarce goods would be distributed fairly to all Americans.

Meat and coffee were at the top of the list, followed by sugar and gasoline; cheese was last. Other items Americans hated giving up were tires, women's stockings, various household appliances, and last, safety pins.

In 1943, the government allocated just 15 percent of the nation's huge steel production to nonmilitary uses. This meant there were no cans for preserving fruits and vegetables. Therefore no canned foods were available on grocery-store shelves. Women had to make daily trips to shops for fresh foods. The visit to one store, however, might turn up no meat and few dairy products. Several more tries might be necessary before the shopper found what she needed.

To increase the availability of fresh food—and therefore decrease the need for steel cans to preserve it— the government advocated that everyone become a small farmer. "Grow a Victory Garden!" the messages proclaimed and suddenly there were small vegetable plots in parks, in vacant lots, and even on city rooftops. The largest gardens provided "keeper plants"—potatoes, carrots, turnips, and squashes—that didn't need to be preserved. Men helped in the gardens, but storing

In New York City's Times Square, two fashion models add their contributions to a huge pile of aluminum cans. A nationwide can drive yielded 20 million pounds, which was badly needed for airplane manufacturing.

and preserving the produce was women's work. Many homemakers experimented with home canning using glass jars and newly developed sterilizing techniques. These processes, however, were not only complicated but dangerous if not done properly.

Housewives also did their part for the war effort by salvaging goods. In this, too, the government had several suggestions. First, it said, do a thorough housecleaning, looking out for anything that can be given up, "Examine the attic, basement, and closets. Old tools. Grandfather's clock, that iron statue . . . you're not using them and the government needs them. Do you know an old flat iron will yield enough for two steel helmets; . . . an old set of golf clubs will furnish enough metal for a .30 caliber machine gun . . . there is enough tin in seventy toothpaste tubes for the radiator of an army truck."

Despite all the scrimping, saving, and pitching in, life was often lonely and sad for women at home, especially for those with very young children. In this letter to her soldier husband, a woman pregnant with her second child and a toddler at home writes, "you're not alone in your restless nights. I don't think I've slept well one single night since you've been gone. . . . Probably I'm more acute to every move Meri makes because I'm in sole charge of her now. . . . Sometimes I get so nervous being with her night and day with no relief."

In a later letter this same woman spills out her money concerns: "My financial worries keep my mind in torment, and added to the strain of missing you, it seems pretty hard. . . . I don't imagine you and I are the only ones having it tough sledding. Probably plenty of your barrack mates are worrying too."

A month later, this woman wrote a very simple letter. It included simply:

Monthly expenditures

Rent	$20.00
Elect.	3.75
Tel.	2.00
Milk	6.50
Laundry	4.00
Groceries	30.00
Insur.	2.95
Range oil	2.80
	72.00

Monthly allowance $80.00. That leaves a balance of $8.00 for clothing, medicine, heat in winter months, newspapers, periodicals, amusement, etc. . . .

I'll give up for tonight and sign off with love.

VICTORY

By 1945 victory in Europe was certain and triumph in Japan was expected as well. Americans at home were finally beginning to look forward to the days after the war when husbands and fathers would come home and life could return to normal. Many women, however, despite the hardships of war, would find it hard to give up the changes they'd made in their lives.

Although American women had taken jobs simply to "do their part," working outside the home had not only helped their country but had increased their self-esteem and self-reliance, too. Many spoke openly of being changed by the experience of earning their own money and making decisions about how they would spend it. Surveys taken in 1945 were revealing. One Gallup poll showed that half of the housewives who had worked during the war wanted to keep their jobs after their husbands returned. Another poll, conducted by the *Ladies' Home Journal,* found that nearly 80 percent of women surveyed thought working was more fun than staying at home.

Yet with war production coming to an end and men returning home, women simply had to adjust to the fact that GI Joe would get the high-paying factory jobs over Rosie the Riveter every time. There would be still be jobs for Rosie, of course, but they would be white- or pink-collar jobs. Some of them, such as bookkeeper, bank teller, and office assistant, would be new for women, because men had held these jobs before the war. As they became "female," however, both the pay and status for such work declined.

Further complicating the picture was the fact that when soldiers returned to resume their "normal" lives, they realized that there was no such thing as "normal" anymore, except perhaps in their memories. Polls of young men found that they overwhelmingly wanted wives who "specialized in homemaking" and who were only slightly updated versions of their own mothers. Less than 10 percent wanted a "business girl who could take care of herself," exactly what most women had become during the war years.

The end of the war, despite the bursts of exhilaration as soldiers returned to their families, was a confusing and unsettling time for many. Men tried to make sense of their war experiences and expected nurturing, indulgent wives and girlfriends to help them. Many women, at the

**Houses in Levittown, Long Island, New York, in 1954.
Suburban developments like this one sprang up
across the nation as men returned to work and
women again became full-time homemakers.**

**An appliance manufacturer's "kitchen of tomorrow"
promised to take the hard work out of homemaking.
Housewives would even have their hands free at
the sink as foot pedals operated the faucets!**

same time, were reluctantly giving up work that had been truly meaningful for them.

The U.S. government set out, once again, to help settle the matter. It offered returning soldiers loans so they could finish their education and improve their professional skills. And it offered low-interest mortgage loans so that young families could buy homes. As millions of couples found their dream houses in the suburbs, far from the work centers, women's employment opportunities decreased even further.

The media also played a key role in nudging wives and mothers back home full time. Pictures of dream houses and dream kitchens, all promising to take the drudgery out of homemaking, appeared everywhere. Yet no appliance or gadget could make full-time homemakers, who yearned for the independence they'd known during the war, feel happy and whole. The divorce rate reached an all-time high in 1946 as confused and disillusioned men and women tried to find happiness.

As postwar life became more complex and perplexing, many Americans looked back on World War II as a time of happy simplicity, when there were fewer options and decisions. Back then men had gone to war to fight an evil enemy; women had stayed behind to work or raise a family, always doing their part. This nostalgic view of the war years has influenced the lives of many Americans for the last fifty years as they have struggled to reconcile reality and illusion.

FOR FURTHER READING

Helmer, Diana Star. *Belles of the Ballpark.* Brookfield, Conn.: Millbrook Press, 1993.

Katz, William Loren. *World War II to the New Frontier, 1940–1963.* Austin, Tex.: Raintree Steck-Vaughn, 1993.

May, Elaine Tyler. *Pushing the Limits: American Women.* New York: Oxford University Press, 1994.

Stein, R. Conrad. *The Home Front.* Chicago: Childrens Press, 1986.

Wright, David K. *A Multicultural Portrait of World War II.* New York: Marshall Cavendish, 1994.

INDEX

ABOUT THE AUTHOR

Susan Sinnott began her publishing career as an editor for *Cricket*, a literary magazine for children. She later worked at the University of Wisconsin Press, where she managed and edited academic journals. Eventually, her own two children pulled her away from scholarly publishing and helped her rediscover the joys of reading and writing books for young people. Ms. Sinnott's books include *Extraordinary Hispanic Americans*, *Extraordinary Asian Pacific Americans*, *Chinese Railroad Workers*, and *Doing Our Part: American Women on the Home Front during World War II*. She lives in Portsmouth, New Hampshire, with her husband and children.